MASTERING
PHYSICS

Understanding Forces *of* Nature:
Gravity, Electricity, *and* Magnetism

KRISTEN PETERSEN

 Cavendish Square
New York

Published in 2015 by Cavendish Square Publishing, LLC
243 5th Avenue, Suite 136, New York, NY 10016

Copyright © 2015 by Cavendish Square Publishing, LLC

First Edition

CPSIA Compliance Information: Batch #WW15CSQ

All websites were available and accurate when this book was sent to press.

Library of Congress Cataloging-in-Publication Data

Petersen, Kristen.
Understanding forces of nature: gravity, electricity, and magnetism / by Kristen Petersen.
p. cm. — (Mastering physics)
Includes index.
ISBN 978-1-5026-0142-1 (hardcover) ISBN 978-1-5026-0143-8 (ebook)
1. Force and energy — Juvenile literature. 2. Gravity — Juvenile literature. 3. Electricity —
Juvenile literature. 4. Magnetism — Juvenile literature. I. Title.
QC73.4 P484 2015
531—d23

Editor: Fletcher Doyle
Senior Copy Editor: Wendy A. Reynolds
Art Director: Jeffrey Talbot
Senior Designer: Amy Greenan
Senior Production Manager: Jennifer Ryder-Talbot
Production Editor: David McNamara
Photo Research by J8 Media

The photographs in this book are used by permission and through the courtesy of: Cover photo and page 1, Igor
Zh./Shutterstock.com; Radu Razvan/Shutterstock.com, 5; Petras Malukas/AFP/Getty Images, 6; ESO/L. Calçada/
File:Artist's impression of the expected dark matter distribution around the Milky Way.jpg/Wikimedia Commons,
11; NASA/AFP/Getty Images, 12; Bridgeman Images, 14; Science & Society Picture Library/Getty Images, 17;
Peter Jackson/Getty Images, 18; Timothy A. Clary/AFP/Getty Images, 21; DanBrandenburg/Getty Images, 22; Alan
Copson/Getty Images, 25; © iStockphoto.com/Bosca78; Richard Kail/Getty Images, 28; © 1991 CERN, 30; Lionel
Flusin/Getty Images, 33; Alison Wright/Getty Images, 34; AP Photo/Czarek Sokolowski, 35; Henning Dalhoff/
Getty Images, 36; © 2013 CERN, 38; Amble/File:South pole spt dsl.jpg/Wikimedia Commons, 40; Bengt Nyman/
File:Nobel Prize 24 2013.jpg/Wikimedia Commons, 42; Pasieka/Getty Images, 43.

Printed in the United States of America

CONTENTS

INTRODUCTION

One afternoon, you and your friends decide to play basketball. You pass the ball to your friend Susan, who makes a three-point shot. The sun is setting, and it starts to get dark, but you all want to keep playing. You turn the court lights on and play for another hour.

You just got some exercise and played a great game of basketball with friends, but you also did so much more. You just interacted with the four fundamental forces in nature.

Susan may have taken the shot by sending the basketball up in an arc, but **gravitational force** pulled the ball down as it passed through the net. Without gravity, the ball would have kept heading upward. Then again, without gravitational force you and your friends wouldn't be playing basketball, you'd be floating away.

Once it was getting too dark to play, electricity was used to turn on the lights. **Electromagnetic force** creates the electricity that powers the lights to make the court bright enough for play after the sun has gone down. While the sun was shining on your game, **weak force**, responsible for radioactive decay, is also responsible for sunlight. The fourth fundamental force of nature, **strong force**, keeps everything in the universe bound together, including the basketball, the court, and you and your friends.

Scientists continue to look into these forces to try to fully comprehend how our universe works. They have been looking back through the window of time, discovering traces of gravitational

The four fundamental forces in nature can be experienced in one game of basketball.

waves and new forces that can explain how our world began. These are puzzle pieces, some revealed only through the use of the world's largest particle collider, that reach back to the beginning of time. What they are learning is testing standard models of physics.

Most people don't ever spend any time thinking about these four forces of nature. However, they are crucial to our world, and understanding their basic concepts helps people comprehend some of the fundamental building blocks of physics.

All objects fall at the same speed, unless one person bounces the ball harder than the next person.

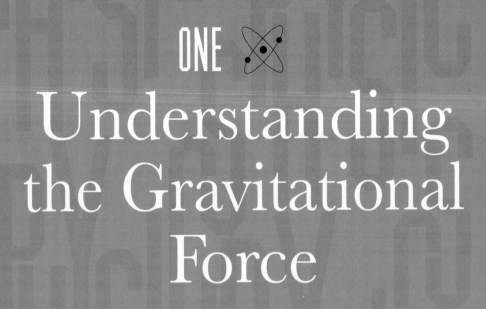

ONE

Understanding the Gravitational Force

f you take off your shoe and then let go of it, it falls to the ground. This action demonstrates the gravitational force, the invisible force that is responsible for the attraction between one object and another. Generally, we just refer to it as gravity. Scientists continue to study the gravitational force, as its laws are still not completely understood.

EARLY STUDIES OF GRAVITY

Observing the effects of gravitation, ancient philosophers believed Earth was the natural resting place of all things. Greek philosopher Aristotle developed a slightly more sophisticated theory, maintaining that objects were pulled to Earth at a speed proportional to their size. A millennium later, legend has it, Italian astronomer Galileo tested this idea by dropping objects of various size from the Tower of Pisa. Galileo concluded that, if the effect of air resistance is eliminated, all objects fall at the same speed regardless of size.

In the late seventeenth century, our understanding of gravitation grew enormously through the work of British philosopher and mathematician Sir Isaac Newton. He studied why the planets in the solar system orbited around the sun in well-defined paths. Newton concluded that an attractive force was acting on the sun and each planet. More importantly, he devised a mathematical expression of this force with his law of universal gravitation.

According to Newton's law, the gravitational force (F) between two bodies (m_1 and m_2) can be calculated using the following equation:

where r is the distance between the two bodies, and G is a

$$F = \frac{Gm_1m_2}{r^2}$$

constant. (Later experiments calculated the value of this universal constant of gravitation as $6.673 \times 10^{-11} N\ (m/k)^2$.)

Newton's law explains that the size of a gravitational force between two objects is proportional to the product of their **masses**. Imagine two objects placed at a set distance from each other. One has a mass of 2 kilograms (4.4 pounds), and the other has a mass of 4 kilograms (8.81 lbs.), so the product of their masses is 8 kilograms (17.6 lbs.). Let's assume the gravitational force between them is equal to one newton. (A newton or N is a unit measuring force.)

Now imagine doubling the size of these two masses, without changing the distance between them. One object now has a mass of 4 kilograms (8.81 lbs.), and the other has a mass of 8 kilograms (17.6 lbs.), so the product of their two masses is 32 kilograms (70.5 lbs.). In the second example, this product is four times larger than that in the first example. By Newton's law, the force between them will be four times larger as well, so the force in the second example has to be equal to four newtons.

Newton's law also indicates that the gravitational force between two objects decreases as the distance between them increases and vice versa. More precisely, the size of the force is the inverse square of the distance between them ($1/r^2$).

This time, imagine two objects set at 1 meter (3.28 feet) apart with a gravitational force of one newton between them. If the distance between them is doubled to 2 meters (6.56 ft.), the force will decrease to 1/4 newton ($r = 2$, so the force equals $1/2^2$, or $1/4$).

What happens if we halve the distance between the two objects? The force will increase to four newtons; $r = 1/2$, so the force equals $1/(1/2)^2$, or $1/(1/4)$, or 4.

POSSIBLE EXCEPTIONS TO NEWTON'S LAW

In the nineteenth century, some astronomical calculations called Newton's law into question. Astronomers found that the orbit of the planet Uranus follows a path different from the one that was charted using Newton's equations. However, this seeming contradiction of Newton's theories soon provided more evidence that the theories were actually correct.

Working independently in the 1840s, two astronomers, John Couch Adams of England and Urbain-Jean-Joseph Leverrier of France, used Newton's law to chart the orbit of an undiscovered planet. Its pull on Uranus could explain the planet's peculiar path. A few years later, German astronomer Johann Gottfried Galle confirmed their speculation by discovering Neptune traveling in the precise path Leverrier had laid out. In the twentieth century, Pluto was discovered in much the same way.

Newton's law of universal gravitation remained unchallenged for hundreds of years. It still ably defines the force of attraction between most objects in the physical world. However, since 1915, when Albert Einstein formulated the general theory of relativity, physicists have realized that under certain conditions the Newtonian law of gravitation no longer holds true. For instance, Einstein's theory is needed to explain the extremely strong gravitational pull between massive objects with little distance separating them.

UNDERSTANDING MASS AND WEIGHT

A planet's gravitational pull on objects on its surface is called **weight**. Weight should not be confused with mass. Mass, the amount of **matter** in an object, is constant. The mass of an object remains the same, regardless of whether the object sits on Earth, on the moon, or on Jupiter.

The Dark Side

From the motion of stars, astronomers have concluded that much of the universe is made up of dark matter. Like ordinary matter, the gravitational force affects dark matter. However, because it does not form stars that emit light, it is invisible, hence its name. While astronomers know dark matter exists through the laws of gravitation, they have yet to determine exactly what it's composed of. They know it behaves differently than the matter that makes up stars, planets, and galaxies, which is collectively referred to as **baryonic matter**. Unlike baryonic matter, dark matter does not absorb or emit light or other forms of electromagnetic **radiation**. For now, scientists are effectively figuring out what dark matter "isn't," but they have yet to figure out what it "is."

Dark matter continues to be studied by physicists and cosmologists. They are trying to figure out how the existing matter in the universe, as well as dark matter and dark energy, can explain how the universe continues to expand. For years, scientists assumed that because gravitational force pulls all objects together, the universe would slow its expansion, and eventually begin to collapse back on itself. However, research has shown that the universe is expanding faster than before, so scientists theorize that dark energy and dark matter must be part of the equation.

The presence of dark matter, shown in blue in this artist's conception of the Milky Way, is thought to be behind unexplained phenomena in our universe.

A man on the moon weighs less and falls more slowly than a person on Earth.

An object's weight can change, however. For instance, an object weighs more on Jupiter than on Earth. Since Jupiter is far more massive than Earth, it has a far greater gravitational pull. Inversely, the same object weighs less on the moon. Since the moon is smaller than Earth, its gravitational pull is smaller as well. As a result, a person could lift huge objects on the moon that he or she could barely move on Earth.

Physicists speak of the strength of a gravitational field in terms of g, which represents the rate of acceleration of a falling object because of gravity. On Earth, g is 9.8 meters per second per second (32.15 ft. per second per second). This means that two seconds after an object is dropped, it will be moving 9.8 meters

Understanding Forces of Nature

per second (32.15 ft. per second) faster than it did at the end of the first second.

At different places on Earth, g is often slightly less or slightly more than 9.8 meters per second per second (32.15 ft. per second per second). The differences are due to variations in the density of Earth's crust. In fact, geologists use the measurement of g to learn about the movements of the crust. On the moon, g is only about 1.6 meters per second per second (5.24 ft. per second per second), while on Jupiter it is about 24.9 meters per second per second (81.69 ft. per second per second).

WAVES AND SATELLITES

On Earth, the gravitational pull of the other bodies in our solar system is most obvious in the behavior of the ocean. The phenomenon of tides results from force exerted by the moon and, to some extent, the sun. In general, the water of the oceans on the side of Earth closest to the moon is pulled up by the moon's gravitational pull, creating a high tide. Our knowledge of gravitation allows us to predict the tidal flow.

Our exploration of space also relies on our understanding of the gravitational force. In order to escape Earth's atmosphere, objects sent into space have to be traveling fast enough to escape its gravitational pull. The laws of gravitation allow us to calculate the necessary speed, known as escape velocity.

Understanding the laws of gravitation also allows us to calculate the exact velocity that artificial satellites need in order to orbit the planet. The calculation must be exact with respect to Earth's gravitational force, as an object moving too slowly would succumb to Earth's gravity and fall back to the planet. Conversely, an object moving too quickly would escape the pull of gravity and head into space. This is similar to the gravitational relationship between the sun and Earth. Earth moves at exactly the correct velocity to keep it orbiting the sun. If it moved any slower, it would be pulled into the sun; any faster, and it would break out of its orbit.

A lodestone was kept on board ships to re-magnetize compass needles. This lodestone box is from the eighteenth century.

TWO

Understanding the Electromagnetic Force

Just as the gravitational force surrounds us, electromagnetic force is also around us at all times. Solid objects keep their form thanks to the power of electromagnetic force. Light is also created by electromagnetic force, as are the electrical impulses our body uses to make our muscles move and think our thoughts.

EARLY UNDERSTANDING OF ELECTRICITY AND MAGNETISM

Since early in human history, the effects of both electricity and magnetism have fascinated people. The ancient Greeks and Romans observed how rubbing certain objects against other objects could create an attractive force, what we now call static electricity. For instance, the Greek philosopher Thales in the sixth century BCE noticed that after he rubbed a wool cloth against a piece of amber, the amber was able to attract lighter objects, such as dust and feathers. Thales incorrectly concluded that the force was a quality of

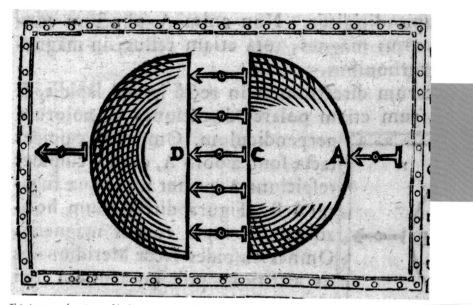

This image of a piece of lodestone (a terrella) cut in half to show the magnetic attraction of Earth appeared in William Gilbert's classic book.

the amber. He did however help give electricity its name, since the Greek word for amber is *elektron*.

The ancients also noted that loadstone, now called magnetite, had the power to attract bits of iron placed near it. The word "magnet" is derived from the fact that loadstone was plentiful in the Magnesia district of Asia Minor. Humans soon also discovered a more useful property of loadstone: If the stone was suspended from a rope or floated on a piece of wood in a pool of water, the stone would orient itself so that one end pointed north. Probably originating in China, very simple compasses based on this principle helped ancient travelers find their way.

At least by the twelfth century CE, sailors used sophisticated compasses to navigate the oceans. By the sixteenth century, it was known that a magnet's attractive powers are concentrated at its two ends, called poles. One pole is naturally attracted to the north, and one to the south. Unlike poles (north and south) of two magnets attract each other, while like poles (north and north, or south and south) repel each other. On a single magnet, the closer the poles are

The Doctor of Magnetism

S ir William Gilbert (1544–1603) was an Englishman who became the physician to Queen Elizabeth, but he is remembered as the man who figured out why magnets work. Gilbert published a six-volume treatise, entitled *On the Magnet, Magnetic Bodies, and the Great Magnet of the Earth*, which consolidated knowledge about magnetism and created new hypotheses on a magnet's properties. He laid out much of the basic terminology used today in electromagnetics.

Gilbert discovered that by rubbing a natural loadstone magnet against an iron bar, he could turn the iron into an artificial magnet. He established the difference between magnetic and static attraction. Most importantly, Gilbert developed a theory about why north poles of a compass point north and south poles point south.

To do his experiments, Gilbert developed an instrument called a versorium that consisted of a suspended metal needle and a round lodestone called a terella. The way the versorium dipped as it was moved around the terella, Gilbert concluded, was analogous to the inclination performed by compass needles at different points on Earth. Therefore, he said that the Earth is magnetic, similar to the lodestone. He also hypothesized that Earth has its own north pole and south pole.

These magnetic poles do not conform with the geographic poles of Earth, so navigators have to make calculations to offset this distance and keep their ships on course.

to each other, the stronger the pull of the magnetic poles will be. (For instance, the pull of the poles of a horseshoe-shaped magnet is naturally stronger than the pull of a bar-shaped magnet's poles.) Furthermore, when a magnet is cut in two, each part becomes a complete magnet, with one north pole and one south pole.

Ben Franklin proved that lightning was a form of electricity.

ELECTRICAL FORCES

By the early eighteenth century, scientists were also developing new theories about electricity. Based on observing simple experiments with static electricity, scientists came to believe there were two separate electrical forces— one that attracted, and one that repelled. Working in England, Stephen Gray found that electrical forces travel through some substances more easily than others. In the United States, Benjamin Franklin's famous kite experiment established that lightning was a natural form of electricity.

A major breakthrough in our understanding of the electric force occurred in 1820. A paper published by Danish physicist Hans Christian Oersted recounted an interesting discovery. He found that if an electric current passed through a wire and that wire was placed near a compass, the compass's needle moved. Oersted concluded that an electrical current could create a magnetic force.

Oersted's discovery led to one of the most important tools of industry, the electromagnet. Winding a coil of wire around an iron bar creates this type of artificial magnet. When a current is sent through the wire, the iron is magnetized. When the current is turned off, the bar loses nearly all of its magnetic force. This allows large electromagnets to pick up large objects, such as cars in a junkyard, and then put them down.

Oersted's work was just as significant for its suggestion that electricity and magnetism were more closely related than previously thought. His work inspired more experiments involving these two forces.

THE ELECTROMAGNETIC FORCE

This study reached a turning point with the work of English physicist Michael Faraday in the 1830s. From Oersted's work, Faraday knew electricity could produce a magnetic effect. Faraday wondered whether the inverse were true—if magnetism could produce an electrical effect. His experiments suggested that electricity and magnetism were in fact different manifestations of one force. Faraday also theorized that electricity and magnetism exerted themselves in invisible "lines of force," suggesting the concept of an electromagnetic field, an area where the magnetic and electrical effects of a moving electric charge are felt.

By the mid-nineteenth century, the experiments of Oersted, Faraday, and others suggested a number of new ideas about electricity and magnetism. In the 1860s and 1870s, the Scottish physicist James Clerk Maxwell brought these together into a coherent theory. He devised a set of equations that mathematically confirmed that electricity and magnetism were a single unified force.

Maxwell also theorized that a magnetic field produced by an **oscillating** electrical charge expands outward at a constant speed. He calculated this speed to be about 300,000 kilometers per second (186,411 miles per second), close to the speed of light. From this, Maxwell hypothesized that light was a form of electromagnetic radiation that travels in waves. His idea also suggested that there were other forms of electromagnetic energy invisible to the eye, thereby predicting the existence of radio waves and X rays.

ELECTROMAGNETISM AT THE ATOMIC LEVEL

Maxwell's theories may be as important to understanding the electromagnetic force as Newton's were to understanding the gravitational force. However, in several ways, the two theories contradicted each other. Inspired to resolve these contradictions, Albert Einstein developed his theories of special and general relativity. While Einstein's work upended Newton's view of the gravitational force, it generally confirmed Maxwell's theories.

During the early twentieth century, advances in particle physics also helped solve remaining mysteries about the electromagnetic force. From Maxwell's time, physicists knew much about how the electromagnetic force functions, but little about why. The answers came with the study of the subatomic particles that make up all matter. Early models of the atom identified three elementary particles. These were the **electron**, the **proton**, and the **neutron**. The proton and the neutron were housed in the atom's nucleus, and the electrons orbited around it.

Physicists found that atoms are held together by the electrical charges of these particles. Electrons have a negative charge, and protons have a positive charge. Neutrons, as the name implies, are neutral, having no charge at all. The unlike charges of the electrons and protons create the electromagnetic force that glues these subatomic particles to one another.

Orbiting electrons, however, are not firmly attached to the nucleus. They might break free from their atom and join another. Electrical charge results from this exchange of electrons. An atom with a deficit of electrons becomes positively charged, while one with an excess of electrons becomes negatively charged.

An electric current is produced when circumstances allow for the free flow of electrons in and out of atoms. In some substances, such as copper and silver, electrons can move easily. They are called conductors. In others, such as rubber and glass, electrons can barely move at all. These are known as **insulators**.

Understanding Forces of Nature

Lightning, here striking New York in July 2014, emits electromagnetic energy.

The phenomenon of magnetism can also be understood in terms of electrons. As they orbit the nucleus, the electrons spin, creating a weak magnetic field. In most substances, half the electrons spin in one direction, while the second half spin in the other, a condition that essentially cancels out the magnetic effect. However, in a few substances, including iron and nickel, the spin of the electrons is not divided equally in the two directions, which makes them easy to magnetize. These substances are called **ferromagnetic**.

Electromagnetic force allows all the atoms in us, and everything around us, to exist. When you see a burst of lightning in the sky or any other visible light, you are seeing the electromagnetic force in action. If you could look inside your body, the chemical reactions constantly going on inside of it would be a further demonstration of the electromagnetic force, and further proof of its importance to all life on the planet.

Lasers are concentrated
electromagnetic waves. They are
used to cut through metal as
well as in laser surgery.

THREE

Taking Advantage of Electromagetism

W hile electromagnetic force is crucially important throughout the natural world, humans have also discovered methods to harness this force in order to successfully power man-made machines and devices. Look around right now, and you will probably see numerous examples of inventions made possible thanks to electromagnetic force, including electric lights, cars, machines, appliances, and so many more.

Most of the magnets we notice in our day-to-day lives perform fairly unexciting tasks, perhaps holding up a note on your refrigerator, or keeping a cabinet door shut. However, hidden from view, magnets are at work in many of the industrial machines and household appliances we routinely use.

Permanent magnets do not require an electrical field, and remain magnetized for a long time. They are used in many types of machinery, including traffic lights, the seismographs that measure the intensity of an earthquake, and the cardiographs that record human heartbeats. They are also found in lathes, conveyors, and hand tools.

Electromagnets are even more prevalent. For instance, every cell phone contains an electromagnet to record the vibrations of the speaker's voice. Nearly everything powered by an electric motor also makes use of an electromagnet. Small electromagnets are found in most factory machinery. Giant electromagnets are used in steel plants and on railroad yards to move heavy loads of steel and iron. In the home, electromagnets make possible a wide array of appliances, such as blenders, washing machines, drills, and shavers, just to name a few.

NUCLEAR ENERGY AND MAGNETS

Magnets play an important role in producing energy in nuclear fusion reactors. Within a reactor, plasma is heated to as high as 100 million degrees Celsius (180,000,032 degrees Fahrenheit). Storing the heated plasma is difficult. At such high temperatures, matter can exist only as charged particles in the center, which would vaporize instantly if they touched the side of a conventional container. Instead, they are stored in magnetic bottles, in which a magnetic field holds the particles, keeping them away from the container's walls.

MODERN USES OF ELECTROMAGNETIC WAVES

In the nineteenth century, our knowledge of the electromagnetic force ushered in the industrial age. In the twentieth century, it spurred another era, the information age. Physicists' understanding of electromagnetic waves paved the way for many revolutionary inventions.

Electromagnetic waves all travel through space at roughly the speed of light. They differ from each other in the frequency at which their electrical and magnetic fields oscillate. This accounts for the different waves on the electromagnetic spectrum, including microwaves, radio and television waves, ultraviolet waves, gamma rays, and X rays.

More recently, scientists have learned how to concentrate electromagnetic waves into laser beams. Lasers are increasingly used in place of knives for surgical procedures. They also use different types of radioactive waves to treat cancer patients.

Friction is reduced in maglev trains elevated by magnetic repulsion.

THE FUTURE OF ELECTROMAGNETIC WAVES

The laws that govern the electromagnetic force have many other practical applications. For instance, the principle that like magnetic poles repulse each other is used in sophisticated rail systems. Through magnetic repulsion, trains are slightly suspended above the tracks, which eliminates friction between the trains and the metal rails. These maglev trains have already been clocked at record speeds of more than 300 miles per hour (482.8 kmh). However, some scientists feel that top speeds of maglev trains could double this number.

Physicists understand that a charged particle moving through a magnetic field will see its movement deflected. Engineers use this principle to make inventions ranging from the television to the oscilloscope work. However, this principle is also important at the microscopic level, as researchers can use these laws to control the motion of a single particle, particularly when traveling in a particle accelerator. Work with particle accelerators has enabled physicists to break apart single atoms as well as their subatomic components. These experiments have enabled physicists to better understand the workings of the universe, and directly led to the discovery of the final two forces of nature.

When current running along this copper wire helps this motor move, it creates an example of turning electrical energy into mechanical energy.

Magnets in Motors and Generators

Nearly any machine powered by an electric motor contains a magnet. Motors operate under the principle of electromagnetic induction. This principle holds that if an electric current flows through a wire and the wire is placed in a magnetic field, the electromagnetic force will cause the wire to move.

When a motor is turned on, current travels along a coil of wire on an axle surrounded by a magnet. Its magnetic field causes the wire and axle to rotate. In this way, the electromagnetic force allows a motor to convert electrical energy into mechanical energy.

Generators convert mechanical energy into electrical energy. In a simple generator, a conductor, often a coil of wire, is rotated between a magnet's poles. The coil passes through the magnetic field, first in one direction, then in the other. As a result, an alternating electrical current, moving in one direction, then the next, flows through the conductor.

In practical terms, the invention of the generator was perhaps the most significant consequence of the discovery of electromagnetism. Generators allow us to easily make use of electricity, an extremely convenient form of energy. Our ability to generate, store, and transmit electricity allows us to operate industrial machinery, light our homes and streets, and operate appliances, computers, televisions, and a host of other electrical devices.

There are several forces that dictate the interaction of atomic and subatomic particles.

FOUR

Understanding Strong and Weak Forces

Through the late nineteenth and early twentieth centuries, physicists were able to study and define two of the fundamental forces, gravitational and electromagnetic. There were theories about two additional forces, the strong force and the weak force, but little was known about either. However, the twentieth century saw the emergence of quantum mechanics. This field of study, which examines how subatomic particles behave, also increased our knowledge of strong force and weak force.

STUDYING STRONG FORCE

The scientific study of atoms as fundamental particles began in the nineteenth century. By the 1920s, physicists determined that atoms were themselves made up of smaller particles. In early models of the atom, these particles were identified as the proton (positively charged), electron (negatively charged), and neutron (neutral charge).

This model, however, created a problem for physicists. By the laws of electromagnetism, the positively charged protons in the nucleus should repel one another. At the same time, of course,

Strong force carried by the gluon

Electromagnetic force carried by the photon

Weak force carried by the W and Z particles

Gravitational force carried by the graviton

quark t   tau neutrino

quark b   tau

quark c   muon neutrino

quark s   muon

quark u   electron neutrino

quark d   electron

Leptons–the electron, muon, and tau– have an associated neutrino and with quarks are considered the elementary particles. They are affected by the strong and weak force.

protons are attracted to one another because of the gravitational force. However, gravitation is a much weaker force than the electromagnetic force. If these were the only forces at work in the atom, no nucleus could hold together for long.

The puzzle was solved as physicists' model of the atom became more sophisticated. They now know that protons and neutrons are made up of still smaller particles called **quarks**. Both protons and neutrons are made up of three quarks each.

Understanding Forces of Nature

Still another particle accounts for the force that attracts the quarks in one proton to the quarks in another. These particles are called gluons. In the exchange of gluons, an attractive force binds the quarks of protons, overcoming the repulsive force of their like electrical charges.

This force that holds the nucleus together is now known as the strong force. It acts across only a very short range, and, as its name implies, it is relatively strong.

WEAK FORCE AT THE SUBATOMIC LEVEL

Like the strong force, the weak force is exerted only on the subatomic level. Like the strong force, physicists theorized its existence long before it could be proven.

In the early years of the twentieth century, the experiments of English physicist Ernest Rutherford indicated that there are three types of radiation, alpha, beta, and gamma. As physicists further studied these phenomena, they found that alpha and gamma radiation could be explained by the laws known to govern the gravitational force and the strong force.

Beta decay proved more of a mystery. A radioactive element experiences beta decay when the nuclei of its atoms are unstable because of an excess of neutrons. As it decays, a neutron spits out a negatively charged electron and, in the process, turns into a positively charged proton. The trouble for physicists, however, was that a certain amount of energy released by the exchange was unaccounted for.

German physicist Wolfgang Pauli first theorized that another, formerly unknown particle was released during beta decay, which would account for the excess energy. Drawing on Pauli's work, Enrico Fermi of Italy dubbed this new particle a neutrino, since it had a neutral charge. He also postulated that there was a fourth force in nature that regulated the transformation of a neutron into an electron, a proton, and a neutrino. In 1959, experiments confirmed the neutrino's existence, validating Fermi's ideas. The fourth force became known as the weak force.

Creating Neutrinos with the W Particle

More recent study of the weak force has revealed that still another particle is involved in beta decay. In the 1970s, physicists theorized that, like the strong force, the weak force requires a force carrier. In 1983, using the CERN particle accelerator in Switzerland, several researchers observed this particle, named the "W" particle after the weak force. Three months later, the CERN physicists found a second particle, the "Z" particle, which is also involved in weak interactions. For their discoveries, they were awarded the Nobel Prize in Physics the following year.

W and Z particles are relatively large. However, the life of W and Z particles is short. They exist for only the fraction of a second needed to fulfill their role in the decay of a particle during a weak interaction.

In beta decay, for example, a neutron (0 charge) first changes into a proton (+1 charge) and a W particle (–1 charge). Almost immediately, the W particle transforms into an electron (–1 charge) and a neutrino (0 charge). The net charge from the decay of the neutron is zero, thereby obeying the fundamental law of physics that calls for the conservation of charge.

This law states that the net charge of an isolated system remains constant unless charge is added or removed from the system. Charge can be created and destroyed only in positive-negative pairs.

The Large Hadron Collider in Switzerland allows researchers at CERN (European Council for Nuclear Research) to track the behavior of subatomic particles.

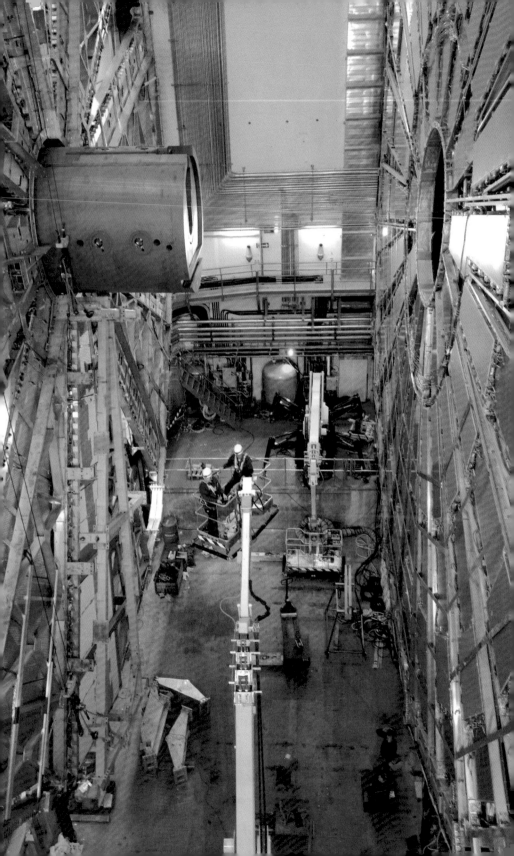

Carbon dating has been used to approximate the age of settlements around Stonehenge.

The weak force may have been responsible for the creation of the stars, planets, and everything else in the universe. Some physicists believe that, when the universe was young, most matter was made of neutrinos. If so, these particles were generated through radioactive decay governed by the weak force.

CARBON DATING AND HYDROGEN FUSION

Weak interactions are relatively rare on Earth, but they do play a role in some familiar phenomena. One instance is radioactive dating, which is used to date ancient objects. Most radioactive dating involves carbon 14, which, through beta decay, turns into nitrogen over time. By measuring the amount of carbon 14 and nitrogen in an object, scientists can determine the object's age. The weak interaction is also responsible for the decay of radon. Decaying radon found in homes has been linked to lung cancer.

Beta decay is not the only effect that weak force has in our world. In fact, its other application is even more important. Hydrogen fusion occurs thanks to the weak force. In hydrogen

Understanding Forces of Nature

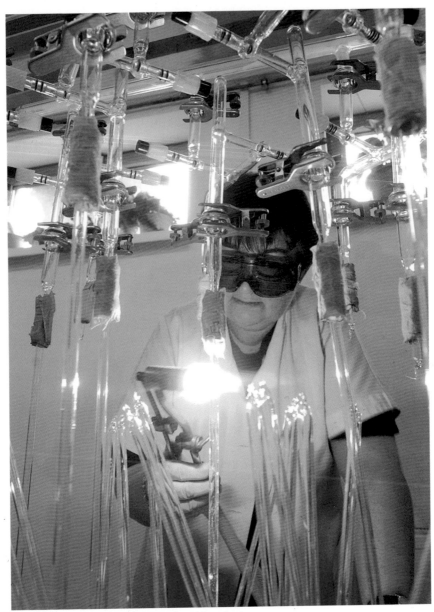

A researcher in Poland measures carbon 14 content.

fusion, four hydrogen nuclei come together to create a hydrogen nucleus, as well as neutrinos. This process of fusion is how the sun is powered, and we all rely on the sun's light and heat, so we rely on weak force as well.

Scientists are still exploring all the factors during and after the Big Bang.

FIVE

Bringing the Four Forces Together

n its birth, the universe expanded from a singular, subatomic point to a small universe about the size of a golf ball. The universe continued to expand outward, an expansion that is still occurring today, thirteen billion years later. At the universe's earliest moments, physicists believed that there weren't four fundamental forces, but only one. Over time, the four forces, gravitational, electromagnetic, strong, and weak, came into being.

Physicists have long tried to turn back the clock, hoping to discover the underlying unity of the various forces of nature. The discovery that electricity and magnetism were the same force was an early step toward unification. In the twentieth century, Albert Einstein attempted to take the next one as he tried to reconcile the laws of gravitation based on his general theory of relativity with Maxwell's laws of electromagnetism. Despite thirty years of effort, Einstein failed to develop a complete unified field theory.

DEVELOPING THE ELECTROWEAK THEORY

In more recent years, however, physicists focusing on unification have made significant progress, making the search for reconciling the four forces one of the most dynamic fields of modern physics.

The greatest success in this field of study was the development of
the **electroweak theory**. In the 1960s, working independently,
three physicists, Sheldon Glashow, Abdus Salam, and Steven
Weinberg, tried to reconcile oddities in our understanding of
the weak force by applying principles derived by the theory of
electromagnetic force. They all were able to show mathematically
that the electromagnetic force and the weak force are different
manifestations of the same force. In 1978, this idea was confirmed
experimentally. Glashow, Salam, and Weinberg won the Nobel Prize
for their pioneering work.

   The electroweak theory helped physicists build the standard
model for particle physics. The standard model is a theory that
describes all known particles and three forces (electromagnetic,

Understanding Forces of Nature

This is an artistic view of the Higgs Field, which is believed to give mass to all matter.

weak, and strong) that act upon them. It established three families of elementary particles, quarks, leptons, and bosons. Bosons are force carriers. The known bosons are the photon (electromagnetic force carrier), gluon (strong force carrier), and W and Z particles (weak force carriers). Physicists postulate the existence of a fourth particle, the graviton, that carries the gravitational force, but it has never been observed.

The electroweak theory, though, also posed plenty of new questions about how two seemingly unrelated phenomena could be unified. For instance, the electromagnetic force works over an infinite range. The weak force, on the other hand, works only over distances smaller than the nucleus of an atom. The disparity in the mass of the two forces' carriers was also peculiar. The photon is massless, while the W and Z particles are among the largest elementary particles.

THE GOD PARTICLE

The difference in the mass of known force carriers was part of a larger question that troubled physicists: Why do particles have any mass at all? One possible answer came from Scottish physicist Peter Higgs in the mid-1960s. Higgs's theory suggested that there is a lattice-like field that fills the universe. As a particle passes through this field, it creates a distortion that gives the particle its mass. The mass of a particle would then depend on how strongly it interacts with this field.

Bringing the Four Forces Together

A Bump in the
Big Bang

The existence of the Higgs boson was proved in 2012 at the Large Hadron Collider located near Geneva, Switzerland.

The collider works by running protons into each other at almost the speed of light. When two W bosons collide, they should scatter in a way that tells scientists how the Higgs boson works. The problem is that this scattering can be seen only in a collision in which both protons emit W bosons. This happens only in one in one trillion proton-proton collisions. In 2014, the ATLAS experiment at the collider observed thirty-four of these collisions.

The discovered properties of the Higgs boson have caused another problem among scientists. They show that the period of rapid expansion after the big bang should have thrown our new universe into chaos, causing a big crunch. This means our universe would have collapsed, only it didn't.

The BICEP2 telescope located near the South Poles detected the presence of gravity waves that could help explain the expansion of the universe. If this discovery is true, something worked to counter the effect of the Higgs boson. Scientists believe they are on the verge of discovering new particle physics beyond the standard model.

New discoveries will be delayed. The Large Hadron Collider was shut down in 2014 so it could be upgraded, and wasn't set to open until 2015.

Peter Higgs put forth the theory of the God Particle, which was seen at the Large Hadron Collider.

In Higgs's theory, this interaction would be governed by a new type of force-carrying particle, now called the Higgs boson. Since this boson would be responsible for all matter in the universe, it has earned the nickname the God particle.

THE GRAND UNIFIED THEORY

Physicists are also close to developing what is called the grand unified theory. This theory would unify not only the electromagnetic force and the weak force, but the strong force as well. The mathematical theories about all three forces show similarities that suggest such a theory might be possible.

Building a theory that unites all four forces presents more of a challenge, since the mathematical structure of gravitation is quite different. Einstein's general theory of relativity remains our best theory for understanding the gravitational force.

Physicists working toward a complete unification theory have some intriguing leads. Of the most promising are five different string theories. All of these theories hold that particles should be seen not as point-like objects, but as vibrating strings. The theories also postulate that the four forces exist in ten dimensions. String theories are attractive to physicists because their mathematical underpinnings seem able to account for gravity. Very recently, evidence suggests that the five string

Understanding Forces of Nature

Superstrings, seen in conceptual computer artwork, are part of Grand Unification Theory.

theories are actually versions of one fundamental theory, now referred to as M-theory.

Physicists continue to search for evidence proving how the four fundamental forces can be unified. With physicists theorizing that strong, weak, and electromagnetic forces all merge at higher energies, only gravitational energy does not fall into this model. However, it's extremely likely that some future physicists will put the pieces together, and change once again our fundamental view of the universe.

GLOSSARY

baryonic matter Matter composed of protons and neutrons; ordinary matter as opposed to exotic forms.

electromagnetic force A fundamental force involving the electric and magnetic effects of particles.

electron A negatively charged particle that orbits an atom's nucleus.

electroweak theory A theory that unifies the electromagnetic force and the weak force.

ferromagnetic Relating to substances, such as iron and nickel, which can be easily magnetized.

gravitational force The attractive force that exists between two objects or particles.

insulator A substance that resists the flow of an electric current.

mass The amount of matter in an object.

matter Something that occupies space, has mass, and exists as a solid, liquid, or gas.

neutron A neutral particle within an atom's nucleus.

oscillating To move in one direction, and then back again many times, or back and fourth as a pendulum does.

proton A positively charged particle within an atom's nucleus.

quark An elementary particle that makes up neutrons and protons.

radiation Energy transmitted as waves, rays, or particles.

strong force The fundamental force that binds neutrons and protons within an atom's nucleus.

weak force The fundamental force that dictates beta decay and hydrogen fusion.

weight The gravitational force of attraction on an object caused by a massive second object.

FURTHER INFORMATION

BOOKS

Bloomfield, Louis A. *How Things Work: The Physics of Everyday Life.* 5th ed. New York, NY: John Wiley & Sons, 2013.

Forbes, Nancy, and Basil Mahon. *Faraday, Maxwell, and the Electromagnetic Field: How Two Men Revolutionized Physics.* Amherst, NY: Prometheus Books. 2014.

Gardner, Jane P. *Physics: Investigate the Forces of Nature.* White River Junction, VT: Nomad Press, 2014.

Knott, Steve. *Isaac Newton: Great Men in History,* vol. 1. Seattle, WA: CreateSpace Independent Publishing Platform, 2013.

WEBSITES

Institute of Physics
www.physics.org

This site provides videos, news, experiments, and databases that can satisfy the curious mind.

SciShow's Videos on the Fundamental Forces of Physics
www.youtube.com/t?list=PLsNB4peY6C6JDc1HcVKjjYzVB0BYEXexd

This YouTube video channel has six video presentations on the four fundamental forces of physics.

The Physics Classroom
www.physicsclassroom.com

This comprehensive tutorial provides instruction for beginning physics students, and is an outstanding resource for their teachers.

BIBLIOGRAPHY

Bloomfield, Louis A. *How Things Work: The Physics of Everyday Life.* 5th ed. New York, NY: John Wiley & Sons, 2013.

Forbes, Nancy and Basil Mahon. *Faraday, Maxwell, and the Electromagnetic Field: How Two Men Revolutionized Physics.* Amherst, NY: Prometheus Books. 2014.

Gardner, Jane P. *Physics: Investigate the Forces of Nature.* White River Junction, VT: Nomad Press, 2014.

Grossman, Lisa. "Higgs Boson Glimpsed at Work for First Time." *New Scientist.* Accessed July 21, 2014. http://www.newscientist. com/article/dn25912-higgs-boson-glimpsed-at-work-for-first-time.html

Halliday, David. *The Fundamentals of Physics.* 10th ed. New York, NY: Wiley. 2013.

Knott, Steve. *Isaac Newton: Great Men in History*, vol. 1. Seattle, WA: CreateSpace Independent Publishing Platform, 2013.

Nave, C. R. "Fundamental Forces." *HyperPhysics.* Accessed July 7, 2014. hyperphysics.phy-astr.gsu.edu/hbase/forces/funfor. html#c1

O'Neill, Ian. "The Higgs Boson Should Have Crushed the Universe." *Discovery News.* Accessed July 17, 2014. news. discovery.com/space/cosmology/the-higgs-boson-should-have-crushed-the-universe-140624.htm

INDEX